Joe & Lorraine,

Celebrate your light
always. I am glad
fate found us...

Michael Williams
2007

IN THE LIGHT OF DAY

IN THE LIGHT OF DAY

A Celebration of Life's Journey

MICHAEL WILLIAMS

To order additional copies of this book, contact:
Xlibris Corporation
1-888-795-4274
www.Xlibris.com
Orders@Xlibris.com
34407

CONTENTS

This book is dedicated to the three most important people in my life:

My wife, Sharon and the inspiration for this book our sons
Matthew Michael and Christopher David.

INTRODUCTION

"In the Light of Day" was born from a collection of experiences, thoughts, hopes and dreams written to capture events and memories of my children's lives. Over the years as family and friends became aware of these poems, I was encouraged to publish them. The poems contained in this book are some of my writings captured throughout those glorious years. They represent the best of my fatherhood memories and most of what I hope all children take with them into adulthood.

I am blessed to have had the opportunity to love and learn through the power of parenthood. This privilege granted me to give and receive has been more than I could have imagined.

This book is a celebration of life's journey.

For Sharon

Dancing
Smiling
They take me places I never imagined
They rain for my sorrow
And gleam like truth on my soul
God bless these eyes that see me
So clearly
God bless these eyes that love me
So fully

ACKNOWLEDGEMENTS

Special thanks to my dad, Levelt David Williams, for being a light in my life. To my mother, Anita, for giving me the freedom to be. To my other mother Iona, thank you for your belief, trust and unconditional love. To my brother Mark—for being a good father and my friend. And to my sister in law, Linda, who can hug you with a smile. To my other brothers, Mark Smith, Larry Foley, Derryn Moten, Chris Matheus and Bob Bolt—thank you hardly seems enough for a lifetime of friendship. A special love is sent to Charrise Smith, Patti Foley, Inga Moten and Andrea Matheus for always standing tall. I am grateful for my oldest friend Cynthia Page and super life teachers like Jim and Pat Sweeney. Michelle and Marci, I am blessed to have walked this journey with you. Thanks to my faith partner Carolyn Eklund. John and Kay Cannon thank you for believing this book possible. It would not have been the same without you. To Nikki Giovanni for her 1996 coffee stained comments of encouragement that will be treasured for life. Uncle Lennie and Aunt Sandra model every day what a loving relationship can be. Thanks to DJ and Barry for the vision and to Yvette, Michael and Saru for encouraging me to color outside the lines. Nancy Beasley and Brad Beasley—I am glad we met. Bob and Bobbie I'm glad we're family. Thank you to my cousins Winnie and Ed for their love. Cousin Sherri, thank you for your constant support and belief in me. And thanks to all of my cousins—especially Glenn, Gerald, Gina, Karen, Denise and Tanya. Much gratitude and love goes out to all of my Aunts, Sylvia, Louise, Maureen, Maxcene, Burnelle and Linda. Thanks also to my Uncles, Donald, Morris and Clarence for showing me the way. I am blessed with many nieces, nephews, godchildren and friends—all very special and too many to name here for fear someone may be forgotten. I do have a special thank you for those who have passed on and whose spirits continue to guide me. Some of those special people are—my great—great grandmother Mimi, my grandparents, Richard and Lillian Williams, Leroy Jones and Louise Jones Thomas, my Aunt Fannie, Aunt Bertha, my dearest uncle O'Dell, Aunt Shirley, Uncle Raymond, Aunt Helen, David Scott, Mr. and Mrs. Alfred Moten and James Bohannan.

A Father's Prayer

I want you to know a world
That accepts your individuality
Without question, without ransom

I hope you know friendships
As deep as roots of a tree
And love as true as that which
Conceived you

I want you to recognize
Hatred
For what it's worth
And never be bribed by its
Ignorance

I pray that we will give you
Confidence and security
To know all is achievable
One
Step
At a time

I pray you will open your
Heart
To know the Lord our
God
And all of his grace

I want you to know the truths of this world
And to love this life in spite of it
As you journey in preparation for the next

GIFTS OF YOUTH

The gifts of youth
Are seen as luck
It's only into the journey
That we know
These gifts come from angels
Watching over us
Blessings from God
And should be acknowledged as such

LOVING GLANCES

Loving glances
Watched in sweet silence
Dances
Often re-enacted
Memories
That slide off eyelashes
Like smiles
That will share these stories
With another willing audience
Someday

For what we forget
Through hurried dawns
And not so quiet twilight
Will be remembered
Lovingly
Always

BE

Be
Triumphant
Let your inner spirit
Be
The outward example
Of who you are
Be
Free
Free enough to fail
And strong enough
To try again
Be
Forgiving
Of yourself
Be
Honest
With yourself
Be
All in the name of
God

Feel Every Moment

Feel every moment
Taste it
Savor it
Capture it in your heart
For however great your memory
That which has passed
Will never be again
However like or similar

The Face of Friendship Knows No Color

The face of friendship knows no color
For they water your dreams all the same
They calm your fears with laughter so
True
It's spiritual
They become you
You become them
And still remain
That individual
Depended upon
With a love so
Quiet
You just have to
Listen

Don't Look Down

Don't look down
Least you forget how graceful
You stroll across this tight rope
Never claiming bravery
You are filled with a spirit
That moves with you
Never swayed
Not even by the wind
For you are stronger
Than you know

READ

Read
To smile
Discover
Learn

Read
To understand
Challenge
Confirm

Read
About different cultures
And far away lands

Read
History
And then read it
Again

THE LENGTH OF DAYS

Your
Distance
Is not
Measured
By miles
Rather by
The length of days
It's taken
To see
You
Eye to eye
You've
Traveled
More
Than half the
Time
We have left
To share
Daily
Or to
Kiss you
Goodnight

THE BULLY

The bully
Sees the
Unique
And
Blazing
Difference
You make
To this
World
The fresh
New perspective
You take
Your brave
Stance
To be
Who you are
I wish
You
Could see
Just how
Afraid
The bully
Is
That you just might
Outshine us
All

FAITH

Faith
Is
Just
Faith
Is
Freedom
Embrace
It
As you glide
Between
What you know
And what you
Believe
To be so

TRUTH

Truth is
Clear
Yet hard to
See
Hard to speak
Hard to hear
Hard to believe

Know that some will
Pick
At your truth
Like birds of
Prey
But live your truth anyway
Breathe it
Believe it
For it is the only clear
Path
To all that matters

SOAR

It is the pain of this
Life
That
Makes
Us
Better
Or
Worse
Choose to
Be
Better
Learn from it
Grow because of it
And then
Set
Yourself
Free
To
Soar

POEM #14

Make
No
Mistake
A victor
Must be declared
For Envy
Walks and
Talks
And always stands
Upright

Poem #15

I love the color of white Dogwoods
That bloom like clouds in the spring
And orange colored skies
That sing lullabies to the sun at the end of the day
And the spirit in your eyes
That dances
Like music notes
Just waiting to be heard

POEM #16

Spread your wings
Over
A magical glory
Introducing yourself
To vivid and imaginative worlds
Full of fantasy
And promise

But beware
Of the non-believers
Always on watch to
Stop
A dreamer

Poem #17

Bend to right
Never to compromise wrong
Embrace what's yours
Love all things well
Know that independence is a
Must
And interdependence sweet joy

Poem #18

There is no
Better time than
Now
To accept God's
Promise
To revel in the beauty
Of you
To share
God's love
And to say out loud
The truth
To know each day
The right road
To happiness
And to take it

POEM #19

Every reality begins
With a
Dream
A peace
Separate from
Reason
Separate from norms
Perfect
And complete

POEM #20

No
Birth order
Or
Station in life
Defines you more
Than your
Hopes
Your
Imagination
Or the passion
That drives you
To know a life
Only
Because you
Believed
It so

POEM #21

It is the unsettled moments
And the uncertain times
We
Survive
That
Define us
Predict us
Sum
Us
And often
Begin
Us

Poem #22

Lay your burdens down
And let the ashes
Burn
Like some smoke
Ascending to
Heaven

Poem #23

Unfortunately
There are no age
Limits
For insecurity
Or
Jealousy
So don't let these sorts
Judge your
State of being
For they are
Shifting shadows
Sent
To confuse you
And conform you
For their own means

MEMORIES

Memories become like
Rich fabric
Over time
Worn
And frayed
Soft
But strong
Forgive time's
Imperfection
It is the familiarity
And not the
Exactness
That will sustain you
And keep you

POEM #25

In the end
It is love
And hocus pocus
Magic wands
And sing-a-longs
Prayers
Colors bright
And neon signs
To roads unknown
That make
Us
Who
We become

Poem #26

There will be days
With no clear path
And no view of the
Horizon
You will have to depend on
Faith
And
Grace
To guide you
Like driftwood
Until smoother water comes along

THIS FAR INSIDE LOVE

One day you will
Fall into her
Eyes
And witness
Miracles
Greater than yourself
Know that days are not even or
Equal
Yet provide the same chance
For honesty

Look for the shade
On a summers day
And learn what it is to be seduced
With a willingness
That will set you free
As you stand upon
A foundation that grows
Stronger and stronger
With every breath

Know that autumn will come
With barren branches
Exposing a freedom
And a promise
That can not be ignored
This far inside love

In the Light of Day

To be loved
Is ordained
But it is the falling
In love
That becomes the witness
To giving
And sharing
Wishing
And hoping
Wanting
And needing
Hurting
And forgiving
It is a miracle
That love
Only remembers
What remains
In
The
Light
Of
Day

Poem #29

Make not
Regret
Your friend
Or occasional associate
But do make introductions to choice
Without making a fool of fate
Close the door to what shines bright
And step confidently into the night

POEM #30

Your soul was
Christened
To travel with mine
At least to overlap in time
You see beauty
And your heart complies
For reason
Confines
Not
Your will
Before you
I knew of no
Gift
This kind

FEAR

Fear
Like
Ghosts
Haunt
Relentlessly
Effortlessly
It never shouts
What a whisper can demand
For once infected
You must obey its command

POEM #32

In the infinite
Wisdom of wonder
There are no
Limits
For an experience
Can not be weighed
Against the next
Or another
Yet to be
Discovered

SECRETS

Secrets
Are like
Diamonds
Seductive for many
And precious to most
Be careful with this
Bounty
For it has weight
Weather receiver
Or giver
It is a treasure
To be guarded

Poem #34

You are a
Dream
No more
Deferred
As waters part
And tears become
Rain
To sacred grounds
Awakening
Spirits
To celebrate
A day
Long to come

POEM #35

Crossing the finish line
Is not
What I applaud
Rather it's the thought
And effort
That envisioned
An accomplishment
And this smile

Poem #36

Be not afraid
Of anyone's prison
You can scale walls and leap from tall buildings
In a single bound
Rejecting all
Requiring chains and self doubt
Because possibilities are what you are about

Poem #37

Family
Is like
An orchestra
No instrument
Greater than the other
No sound
Sweeter
Than being on time
For what we start
Should be finished together
Otherwise
Everything in between
Has no
Matter